Tiny Workers

Ants in Your Backyard

Written by Nancy Loewen
Illustrated by Brandon Reibeling

Backyard Bugs

Thanks to our advisers for their expertise, research, knowledge, and advice:

Gary A. Dunn, M.S., Director of Education
Young Entomologists' Society
Lansing, Michigan

Susan Kesselring, M.A., Literacy Educator
Rosemount-Apple Valley-Eagan (Minnesota) School District

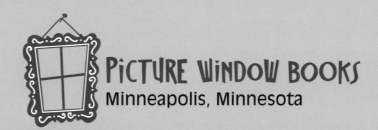

PicTURE WiNDOW BOOKS
Minneapolis, Minnesota

Managing Editor: Bob Temple
Creative Director: Terri Foley
Editors: Brenda Haugen, Nadia Higgins
Editorial Adviser: Andrea Cascardi
Copy Editor: Laurie Kahn
Designer: Melissa Voda
Page production: Picture Window Books
The illustrations in this book were prepared digitally.

Picture Window Books
5115 Excelsior Boulevard
Suite 232
Minneapolis, MN 55416
1-877-845-8392
www.picturewindowbooks.com

Printed in the United States of America.

Library of Congress Cataloging-in-Publication Data
Loewen, Nancy, 1964–
Tiny workers : ants in your backyard / written by Nancy Loewen ; illustrated by Brandon
Reibeling.
p. cm. — (Backyard bugs)
Summary: Describes the physical characteristics, life cycle, and behavior of ants.
Includes bibliographical references (p.   ) and index.
ISBN 1-4048-0141-3 (hardcover)
1. Ants Juvenile literature. [1. Ants.] I. Reibeling, Brandon. II. Title.
QL568.F7L65 2003
595.79'6—dc21
                                                                      2003006096

Table of Contents

A-Mazing Little Homes

Look! Down there on the sidewalk. What is that little pile of dirt?

Take a closer look. What insects do you see moving in and out of the dirt? That's right—ants! The dirt is like the door to their house.

The ants that make these little piles of dirt are pavement ants. They often build their homes beneath cracks in sidewalks and driveways. Every anthill we see has a maze of tiny tunnels and caves below it.

6

Ants are social insects. They live in groups called colonies and work together as a team.

There are more than 11,000 kinds of ants. They live all over the world, except where it's very cold. They usually build their homes in soil, dead trees, or rotting leaves.

What Do Ants Eat?

Look at that ant. What is it carrying? It looks like a piece of potato chip. The potato chip is bigger than the ant!

Ants eat lots of things, such as food scraps, seeds, and dead insects. They spit a special juice on their food to turn it into liquid. Then they drink their meal.

The liquid goes into a little storage sac called a crop. The ant can store food for itself or share it with others. If you ever see ants that look like they're kissing, they are probably sharing food.

Queen Ants

What is that insect? It looks like an ant,
but it's bigger and has wings. It must be
a queen ant. Male ants have wings, too,
but they are smaller than queen ants.

You won't see queen ants or male ants
very often. They only leave their
colonies during mating season.
Their mating season is just a few days
in early spring or late summer.

When it's time to mate, queens and males leave their colonies and fly high in the air. This is called a wedding flight. The ants usually mate while flying.

11

Starting a Colony

After mating with a male ant, the queen can lay eggs. Her job is to start a new colony.

She digs a small tunnel in the ground and lays her eggs. A queen ant lays 10 to 20 eggs when she first starts a colony.

As the colony grows, the queen lays more eggs. Queen ants usually live from 3 to 10 years. They are the only ants that lay eggs.

The eggs hatch in about 25 days. The young ants look like fat, little worms. They are called larvae.

The queen feeds the larvae with a special liquid from her body. All the larvae do is eat and grow.

New Workers

After a couple of weeks, the larvae spin silk over their bodies and form cocoons. They are now called pupae. You can't see it, but there is a lot going on in the cocoons. The pupae are turning into adults. The pupae will leave their cocoons in about 25 days.

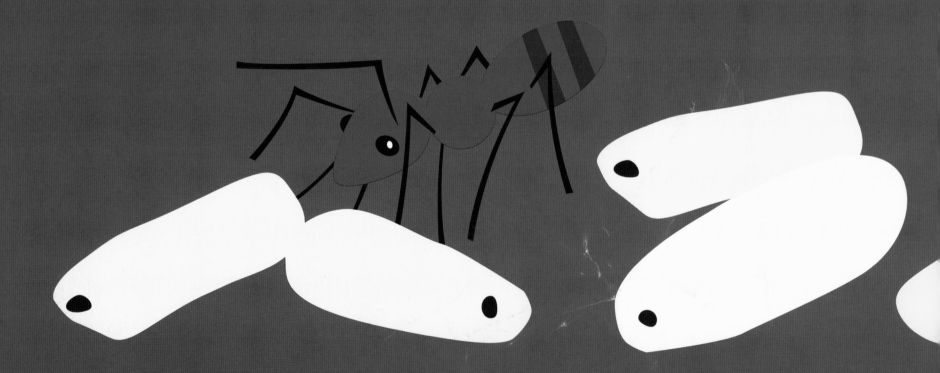

The first ants to hatch in a new colony are all worker ants. They are female ants that don't have wings. The worker ants take care of the colony.

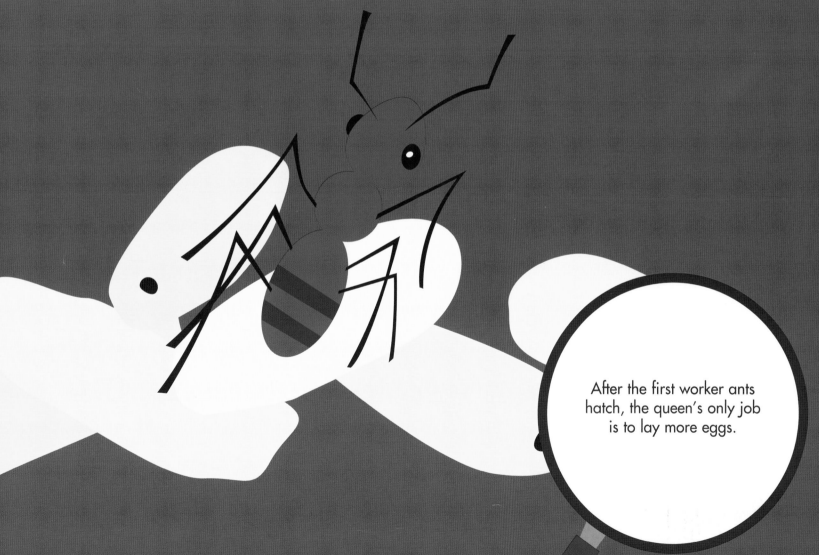

After the first worker ants hatch, the queen's only job is to lay more eggs.

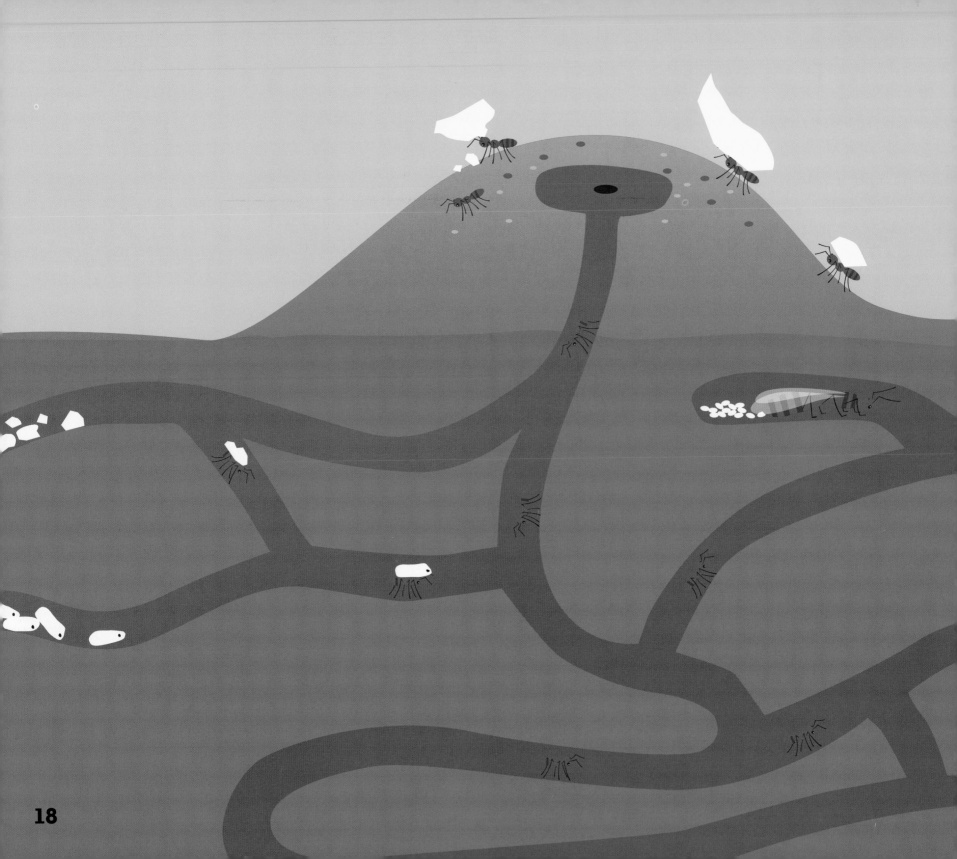

Worker ants have different jobs. Some take care of larvae and pupae. Some fix tunnels and take out empty cocoons. Others go out and bring back food to the rest of the colony.

In larger colonies, some ants become soldiers. They fight against insects and other ants to keep the colony safe.

Worker ants lick pupae and larvae, covering them with a special kind of substance. The substance kills germs and keeps mold from growing.

Ants and People

Ants and people don't always get along. Ants sometimes get into houses in search of food. They also can hurt some farm crops. But ants do good things, too. They loosen the soil, which helps keep plants healthy. They eat some insect pests and are great at cleaning up food scraps.

What's another good thing about ants?

They're fun to watch!

Look Closely at an Ant

An ant's **antennae** are bent in the same way your arm bends at the elbow. Ants use their **antennae** to taste, smell, and touch. They even talk to one another by touching their **antennae** together.

An ant's jaws, or **mandibles**, have tiny, sharp teeth. They are perfect tools for cutting, digging, or carrying things.

Ants have compound **eyes**. Compound **eyes** are made up of lots of pieces, called lenses.

Ants can carry things with their **legs**.

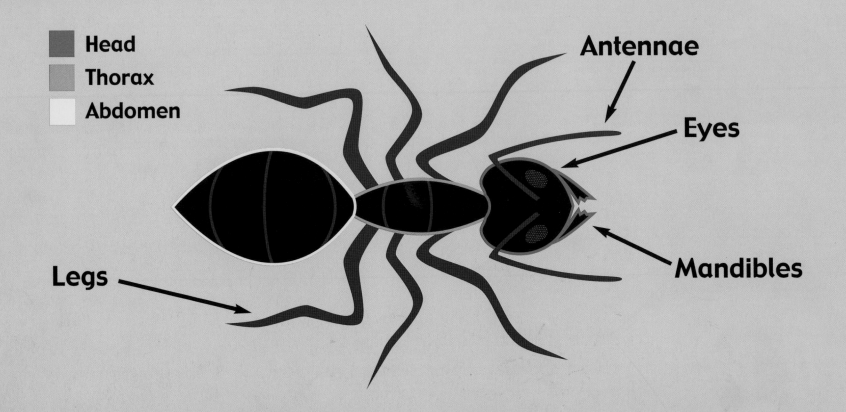

Head
Thorax
Abdomen

Antennae

Eyes

Mandibles

Legs

- Ants are very strong. They can carry objects that are up to 50 times their own weight!

- Ants can control which kind of ant will hatch from an egg. They create a queen by choosing a larva and feeding it special food. Once a year, queens lay some unfertilized eggs, which become males.

- In the winter, ants seal the entrance to their nest and go to the deepest, warmest part of it. They don't eat until spring.

- When ants find a large source of food, they go back to the nest to tell the others. They leave a trail of odors so they can easily find their way back to the food.

- Sometimes ants form huge colonies, which are made up of many smaller colonies that work together. These supercolonies can cover 1 square mile (2 1/2 square kilometers) and contain 300 million worker ants!

Make an Ant Farm

You can make your own ant farm and watch ants up close! You'll need a glass jar with the label removed, dirt, ants, a sheer knee-high nylon stocking (make sure to ask if you can use it), a rubber band, and brown or black paper.

Fill the jar with loose dirt. Put the ants in the jar. Cover the jar with the nylon stocking, and put the rubber band around the top. If the stocking is too big, you can trim it. Tape the paper around the jar so it will seem dark, like the jar is underground. The ants probably will start building tunnels in the dirt. You can take the paper off every few hours to check on them. Be sure to put a little food and water in the jar, too. And get out your magnifying glass so you can see just how amazing these insects are!

antennae – Antennae (an-TEN-ee) are feelers on an insect's head. Antennae is the word for more than one antenna (an-TEN-uh).

larvae – Larvae (LAR-vee) are newly hatched ants. They look like little worms. Larvae is the word for more than one larva.

mate – Male and female ants mate by joining together special parts of their bodies. After they've mated, the female can lay eggs.

pupae – When insects are pupae (PYOO-pee), they are changing from larvae to adults. These changes take place in cocoons, or cases. Pupae is the word for more than one pupa (PYOO-puh).

silk – Silk is long, thin threads that stick together to make a cocoon.

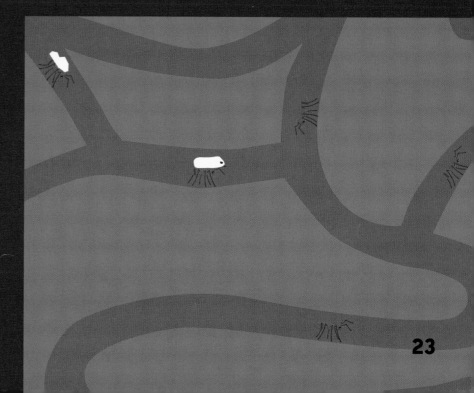

To Learn More

At the Library

Allen, Judy. *Are You an Ant?* New York: Kingfisher, 2002.

Christian, Eleanor. *Looking at Ants.* Mankato, Minn.: Yellow Umbrella Books, 2000.

Hartley, Karen. *Ants.* Des Plaines, Ill.: Heinemann Library, 1998.

Heinrichs, Ann. *Ants.* Minneapolis: Compass Point Books, 2002.

On the Web

enature.com
http://www.enature.com/guides/select_Insects_and_Spiders.asp
Articles about and photos of almost 300 species of insects and spiders

The National Park Service
http://www1.nature.nps.gov/wv/insects.htm
A guide to finding and studying insects at national parks

University of Kentucky Department of Entomology
http://www.uky.edu/Agriculture/Entomology/ythfacts/entyouth.htm
A kid-friendly site with insect games, jokes, articles, and resources

Fact Hound
Fact Hound offers a safe, fun way to find Web sites related to this book. All of the sites on Fact Hound have been researched by our staff.
http://www.facthound.com

1. Visit the Fact Hound home page.
2. Enter a search word related to this book, or type in this special code: 1404801413.
3. Click on the FETCH IT button.

Your trusty Fact Hound will fetch the best sites for you!

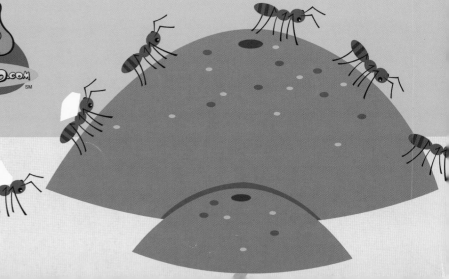

Index